Oxford
International
Resources

1

English
Workbook

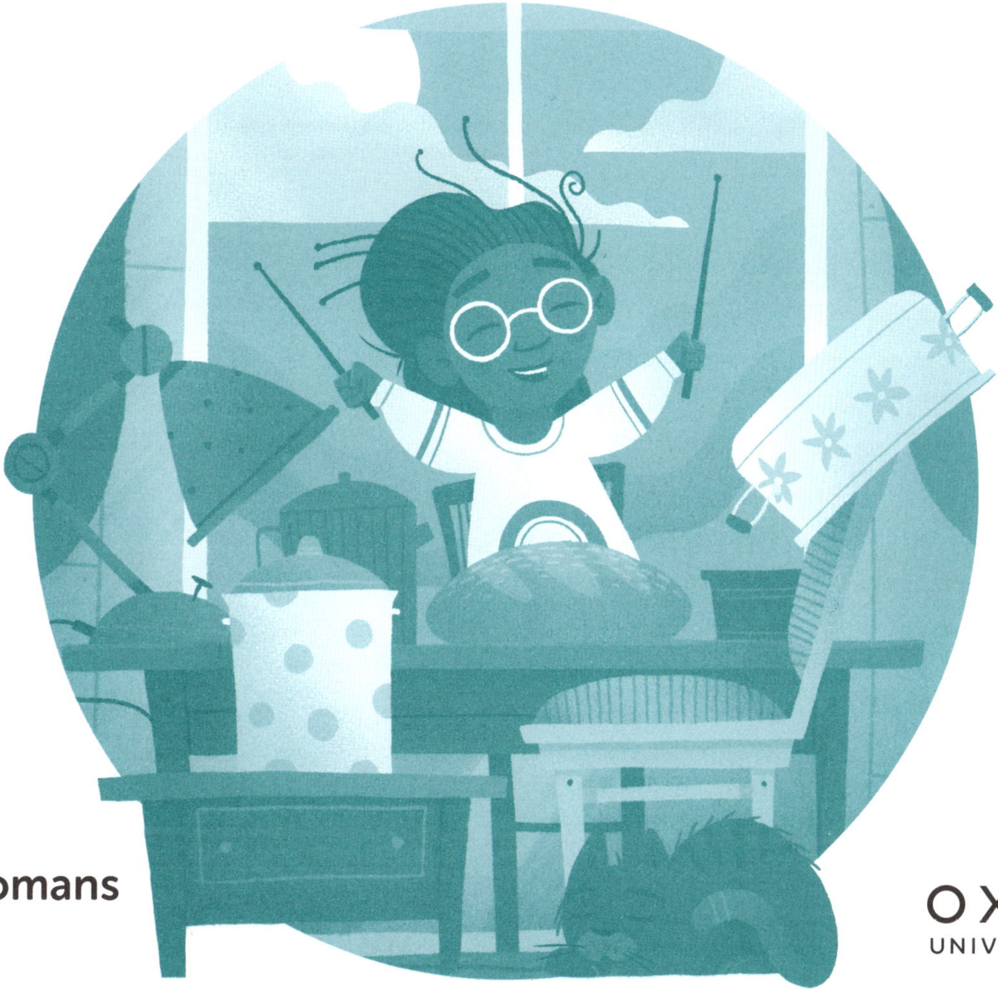

Anna Yeomans
Liz Miles

OXFORD
UNIVERSITY PRESS

OXFORD
UNIVERSITY PRESS

Great Clarendon Street, Oxford, OX2 6DP, United Kingdom

Oxford University Press is a department of the University of Oxford. It furthers the University's objective of excellence in research, scholarship, and education by publishing worldwide. Oxford is a registered trade mark of Oxford University Press in the UK and in certain other countries

British Library Cataloguing in Publication Data

Data available

978-1-38-202003-9

10 9 8 7

Paper used in the production of this book is a natural, recyclable product made from wood grown in sustainable forests. The manufacturing process conforms to the environmental regulations of the country of origin.

Printed in India by Multivista Global Pvt. Ltd

Acknowledgements

The publisher and authors would like to thank the following for permission to use photographs and other copyright material:

Cover: Artwork by Dan Gartman. **Photos: p3(a):** Andrea Slatter/Shutterstock; **p3(b):** Krzysztof Odziomek/Shutterstock; **p82:** Butterfly Hunter/Shutterstock; p85: Steve Cox Illustration/Oxford University Press.

Artwork by Dan Gartman, John Abbot Nez, Micha Archer, Marcin Piwowarski, Jan Smith, Meilo So, Francois Ruyer, Hannah Cummings, Alex Brychta, Alex Steele-Morgan, Mona Meslier Menuau, and Q2A Media Services Pvt. Ltd.

Rob Alcraft illustrated by Mona Meslier Menuau: *When Crow Ate My Sandwich* (Oxford Reading Buddy, OUP, 2020), reprinted by permission of Oxford University Press.

John Foster: 'Poppadoms', first published in *Oxford Reading Tree: Food Poems* compiled by John Foster (OUP, 1993), copyright © John Foster 1993, reprinted by permission of the author.

Richard James: 'Today I'm a Drummer' first published in *Oxford Reading Tree, Music Poems* compiled by John Foster (OUP, 1996), reprinted by permission of the author, Richard Edwards.

Laurie Krebs: *Off We Go To Mexico! An Adventure in the Sun* (Barefoot Books Ltd, 2006), text copyright © Laurie Krebs 2006, reprinted by permission of Barefoot Books, Inc.

Any third party use of this material, outside of this publication, is prohibited. Interested parties should apply to the copyright holders indicated in each case.

Every effort has been made to contact copyright holders of material reproduced in this book. Any omissions will be rectified in subsequent printings if notice is given to the publisher.

The manufacturer's authorised representative in the EU for product safety is Oxford University Press España S.A. of el Parque Empresarial San Fernando de Henares, Avenida de Castilla, 2–28830 Madrid (www.oup.es/en).

Contents

1 At home

A Draw a picture of you with your family.

B Write their names here.

_____

_____

Learning tip
Remember that names begin with a capital letter.

My toy

A Draw a picture of you with your favourite toy at home.
Then write the word.

I am playing with my _____.

Lost things

1 Mina has lost a shoe again. Find it and circle it.

2 Harry has lost a cup. Find it and circle it.

B Where would you put these things so they are not lost? Draw them in the picture.

wool   book   pen   cushion   doll

C Look at the picture at the bottom of page 6, then read the words and sentences below.

1 Complete the sentences by choosing the correct object.

wool   **book**   **doll**

cushion   **pen**

The _____ is on the bookshelf.

The _____ is on the sofa.

The _____ is in the basket.

The _____ is in the pot.

The _____ is in the toy box.

2 Add one more object to the sofa and write a sentence about it.

The _____ is _____

the sofa.

Lost and found

A Draw a line to link the person to the thing they have lost.

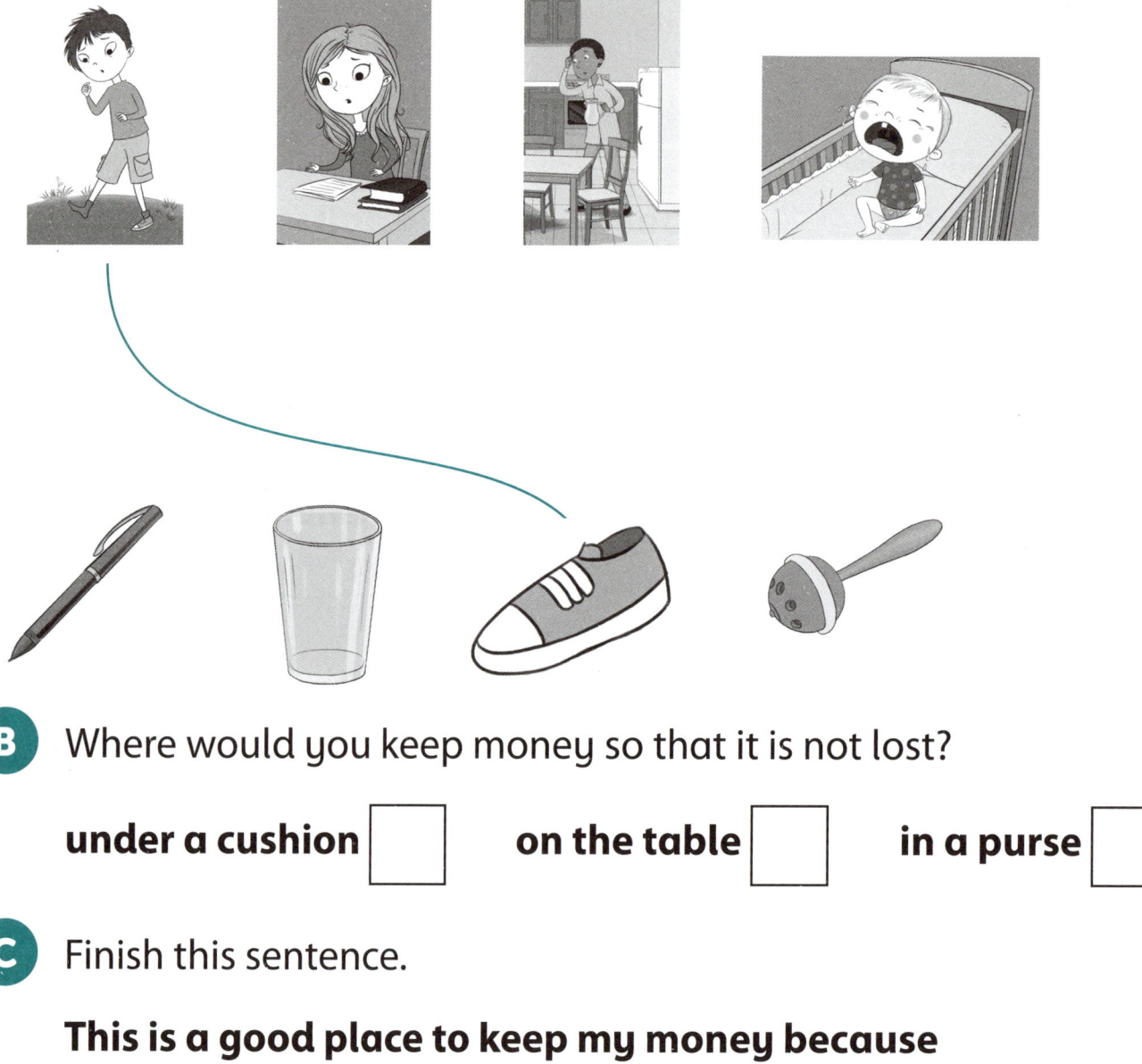

B Where would you keep money so that it is not lost?

under a cushion ☐   **on the table** ☐   **in a purse** ☐

C Finish this sentence.

This is a good place to keep my money because

_____

_____

Writing names

A Write your name. Start with a capital letter.

_____

B When you are at home, who helps you to find your lost toy?
Draw their picture.

C Write a sentence about your picture. Don't forget the full stop.

This is _____

Word detective

A

1 Find these words in the word search and circle them.

> **comic   book   shoe   pen   teddy**

c	o	m	i	c	t
f	k	s	h	o	e
b	o	o	k	v	d
p	p	e	n	z	d
r	w	c	c	m	y

Learning tip
Look for letters down the box as well as across the box.

2 Read the words aloud. Write the word with the /**sh**/ sound.

_____

B Circle the letters that should be capital letters and add a full stop to each sentence.

mina looked under the sofa

mum came to help

i can see grandma's glasses

she looked behind the curtains

C Choose a word to finish each sentence.

under   behind   on   up

It is _____ the table.

He is _____ the ladder.

Sit _____ the sofa.

I am _____ the curtain.

Get writing

Choose the correct words to complete the sentences.

Mina

sofa

hat

Mum

Grandpa lost his

_____.

Harry looked under the

_____.

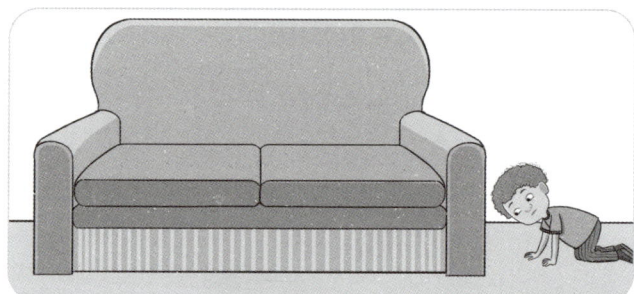

_____ **looked**

in the drawer.

Harry found it.

_____ **had it!**

Check my learning

Unit 1 At home

Name _____ Date _____

☺ I understand and can do this well.

😐 I understand but I am not confident.

☹ I don't understand and this is difficult.

Learning objective	☺	😐	☹
Reading skills			
I can use my knowledge of letters and sounds to read words.			
I understand the meaning of 'lost' and 'found'.			
I can find and write a word that has the /**sh**/ sound.			
Writing skills			
I can hold a pencil to draw and write.			
I know that names start with a capital letter and the word 'I' is a capital letter.			
I can write simple sentences and add full stops.			
Language (spelling) skills			
I can choose and spell words correctly to complete sentences.			

2 Show me, tell me

Signs and labels

A Colour the signs. Tick the signs that tell you to do something.

B Draw a sign you have seen, then colour it in.

C Talk with a friend about what your sign means.

A Help Shari put the things away.
Draw a line from each object to the correct box.

Glue

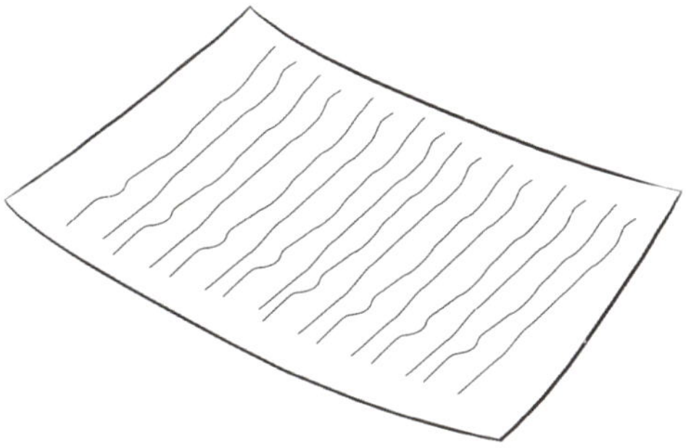

Paper

Books

B Read the colour labels. Colour them the correct colours.

red

green

yellow

blue

Word detective

A Underline the words that begin with 'p'.

pen   scissors   ink   paper   Maths   paint

B Write the missing letter of each word on the signs.

S e t

☐top

Turn the
☐ap off

No
☐ntry

Our senses

A Our five senses are sight, hearing, taste, smell and touch.
Look at the pictures. Which body part goes with which sense?

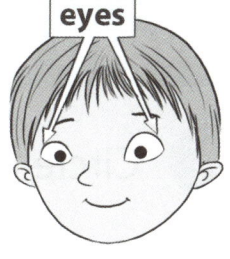

sight	hands
hearing	nose
taste	eyes
smell	tongue
touch	ears

B Find the words for the body parts in the word search.

m	n	o	s	e	t
d	h	s	n	m	o
h	a	n	d	s	n
p	e	y	e	s	g
w	x	n	t	m	u
e	a	r	s	q	e

Word detective

A Circle the word that has the /**ch**/ sound.

> **taste   touch   smell   hear**

B Draw lines to link the words that rhyme.

hear	**touch**
fell	**fear**
look	**smell**
much	**book**

C

1 Write a label for this picture. It rhymes with **band**.

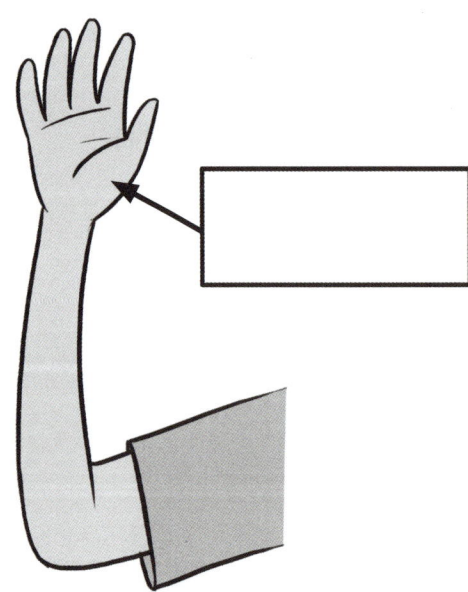

2 Which of the five senses do we use our tongue for?

Labels

A Read the words in the box.

> **face   head   eyes   nose   mouth   chin**
> **leg   arm   foot   hand   ears   chest**

Which parts of the body are they? Point to the body parts on the diagram.

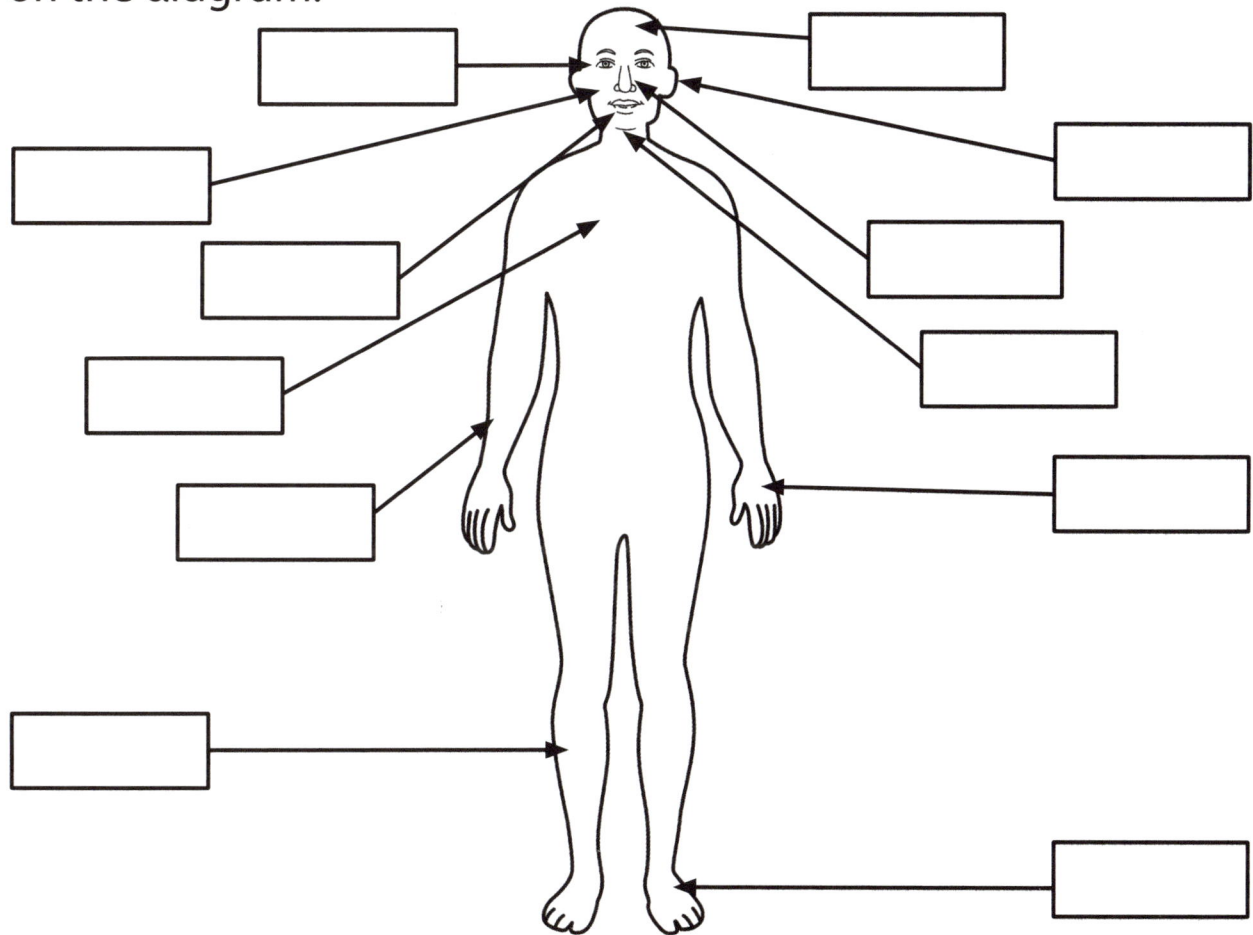

B Write each word in the right place on the diagram.

C Say the words aloud. Which words start with the /**ch**/ sound?

Practise writing **ch**: _____

Word detective

A Read these words aloud.

jump

run

skip

play

eat

sleep

B What do we call a **doing** word?

_____

C Complete the missing letters in these **doing** words.

p _ _ y   j _ mp   _ _ ip   e _ t   sl _ _ p

A Which of these things help you to stay healthy?

playing football ☐

watching TV ☐

sleeping ☐

skipping ☐

eating fruit ☐

Which of these things do you like to do? Tell a friend why you like it.

B Finish the sentence. Don't forget to add a full stop at the end.

I like _____ because

_____

Get writing

Part 1

Write some signs to put around the classroom.

Make sure each sign has a picture and a word.

Part 2

What sign would you like to put up at home?

Write and draw a sign for your home.

Part 3

Write a list of the things you need to stay healthy.

Check my learning

Unit 2 Show me, tell me

Name _____   Date _____

☺ I understand and I can do this well.

😐 I understand but I am not confident.

☹ I don't understand and this is difficult.

Learning objective	☺	😐	☹
Reading skills			
I can talk about the meaning of a sign near me.			
I can find words that begin with the same sound.			
I can link words that rhyme.			
I can find a word that has the /**ch**/ sound in it.			
Writing skills			
I can answer questions by ticking the correct answers.			
I can finish a sentence and add a full stop.			
I can write a list of the things I need to stay healthy.			
Language (spelling) skills			
I can write a word that rhymes with 'hand'.			
I can add missing letters to spell words.			

3 Everyday poems

Read this poem out loud.

Bap-bop

Bap-bop
Bat the ball.
Bap-bop
Over the wall!

Thank you!

Bap-bop
Bat it, bop it
Bap-bop
The ball is back!

A Where did the ball go?

over the wall ☐ under the wall ☐ up a tree ☐

B How did the ball get back to the girl?
Tick the correct answer.

It bounced back from the wall. ☐

The boy hit it back to her. ☐

A dog took it back to her. ☐

C This poem uses the nonsense words **bap-bop**.
Read it again. What do you think bap-bop sounds like?

the wall ☐ the boy ☐ the ball ☐

Learn this poem. Say it to a friend out loud.

Today I'm a drummer

Today I'm a drummer,
I'm drumming everywhere,
I'm drumming on the table-top,
I'm drumming on the chair,
I'm drumming on the biscuit tin,
I'm drumming on the bread,
I'll drum my drums till evening comes,
And then I'll drum in bed.

Richard James

Word detective

A

1 Write the word from the poem that rhymes with **bread**.

_____

2 Find words from the poem that begin with /**b**/. Write them down.

_____

> **Learning tip**
> Words that rhyme sound the same, like 'fun' and 'run'.

B What does **till** mean? Tick the correct answer.

now ☐   until ☐   before ☐

C Find these words from the poem in the word search.

| tin | on | and | drum | chair |

d	f	z	t	u
j	o	z	i	t
a	n	d	n	h
d	r	u	m	e
c	h	a	i	r

Read the words you have found.
Underline the word with the /**ch**/ sound.

27

Read this poem to an adult or a friend.

Poppadoms

Poppadoms, poppadoms,
plain or full of spice.
Poppadoms, poppadoms,
with chicken and rice.
Crispy hot poppadoms
to crunch and chew.
A plateful of poppadoms
just for me and you.

John Foster

A What foods are named in the poem?

_____

_____

B

1 Ask a friend or an adult about their favourite food.
Why do they like it?

2 Tell them about your favourite food and why you like it.

C

1 Draw a picture of your favourite food.

_____

2 Write a sentence to describe it.

_____

_____

Get writing

Part 1

Write the missing words to finish the poem.

> **by the wall**   **on my chair**   **at my school**

Today I'm a singer
I'm singing in the hall

I'm singing _____

I'm singing by the pool

I'm singing _____

I'm singing _____
I'm singing everywhere!

> **Language tip**
> When you have finished, read the poem. Does it sound good? If not, try swapping some of the words.

Part 2

Now think of two other places where you can sing and write these below. Use the words in the box to help you.

> **under**   **next to**   **behind**   **on top of**

I'm singing _____

I'm singing _____

Check my learning

Unit 3 Everyday poems

Name _____   Date _____

☺ I understand and I can do this well.

☻ I understand but I am not confident.

☹ I don't understand and this is difficult.

Learning objective	☺	☻	☹
Reading skills			
I can find words that begin with the same sound.			
I can find words with the /**ch**/ sound.			
I am learning to sound out and remember new words.			
Writing skills			
I can answer questions by ticking the correct answers.			
I can write new lines for a poem.			
Language (spelling) skills			
I can find and spell rhyming words.			
I can learn new words from a poem.			

4 Make the world a better place

When Crow Ate My Sandwich

This is Crow. I've known him since he was tiny.

If I find Crow something nice, he brings me a present in return. He holds his wings out wide and makes a little **bow**. He's a very **polite** crow.

This morning he brought me a beautiful button. He loves collecting shiny things.

Dad doesn't really like Crow, which is a shame. I think it's because Dad is always out at work. He knows Crow is at home, eating his plants.

Dad always shoos Crow away and says "Get off my flowers!".

A What does Crow bring the girl?

a plant ☐   a hat ☐   a button ☐

B Circle the words that describe what Dad thinks of Crow at the beginning of the story.

polite   annoying   bad   fine   helpful

C What does Crow like to collect?

_____

Today, Dad is cross. He's lost his keys.

Suddenly, I have an idea. I think Crow can find Dad's keys.

"Crow," I say, "this is **serious**."

"Shiny," I say.

"Keys," I say.

I show him the door key, and I know that Crow understands.

Then I give Crow my *whole* sandwich.

Crow eats my sandwich, and then he disappears. I wait for him to come back, but he doesn't.

Now I know that Crow didn't really understand; it was just me being silly.

It's early, but I'm going to bed. I say, "Night, Dad," but Dad says, "Is that your crow?"

And then Crow is here. He's back, hopping in through the window. He's holding something in his beak. Dad's shiny keys!

Crow looks at Dad carefully. Then he makes a little bow. He's a very polite crow.

Suddenly, Dad smiles. "You are a very fine bird," he says. "You are my favourite crow."

When Crow Ate My Sandwich

A What did the girl ask the crow to find?

a sandwich ☐   Dad's keys ☐   Dad's plants ☐

B Circle the words that describe what Dad thinks of Crow at the end of the story.

polite   annoying   bad   fine   helpful

C What did Crow do to help Dad?

_____

_____

Story review

 A

1 Draw a picture of your favourite part of the story.

2 Say or write why you like this part.

I like the part where

_____

because

_____

_____.

B

1 Did you like the story *When Crow Ate My Sandwich*? Tick a box.

I liked it ☐   **I did not like it** ☐

2 Write what you liked or didn't like about the story.

_____

_____

C

1 Who helped whom in the story?

_____

2 Dad's opinion of Crow changed by the end of the story because Crow helped him. Have you ever helped someone?
Write a sentence to say what you did.

_____

_____

_____

_____

Word detective

A

1 Find these words from *When Crow Ate My Sandwich* in the word search.

| present | button | plants | cross | keys | beak |

p	r	e	s	e	n	t
l	a	y	l	t	r	k
a	c	b	e	a	k	e
n	r	a	t	t	f	y
t	b	c	r	o	s	s
s	u	m	l	p	t	s
b	u	t	t	o	n	s

2 Which word means the same as **gift**?

What is another word for **cross**?

B

1 Find words with the /**oo**/ sound in the middle. Circle them.
Then write an /**oo**/ word of your own.

good   loves   crow   shoos   looking   (**oo**)

_____

2 Find words with the /**ow**/ sound at the end. Circle them.
Then write an /**ow**/ word of your own.

crow   good   know   peas   home   (**ow**)

_____

C Complete these sentences using words from the story.
Try not to look back at the story!

One day, Dad lost his _____ . I asked _____ to

find them. Crow ate my _____ and then went off

to find Dad's keys. Crow was gone for a long time. Then

Crow came back with _____ keys. Crow gave Dad a little

_____ . Dad said he thought Crow was very _____ .

Get writing

Language tip
There is one full stop and three capital letters.

Part 1

The words in the box make a sentence. Write the sentence. Add the missing full stop and capital letters.

> crow flew back home with Dad's missing keys

_____

_____

Part 2

How did the girl in the story make the world a better place? Write a sentence.

_____

_____

_____

Write a story

Part 3

Think about a time when you helped someone. Fill in the gaps to write the beginning of a story about making the world a better place for a friend or family member.

One day, on my way home from school, I saw _____.

_____ **was upset because** _____ **. I knew**

straight away how I could help. I _____.

Draw a picture to go with your story.

```




```

Check my learning

Unit 4 Make the world a better place

Name _____   Date _____

☺ I understand and I can do this well.

😐 I understand but I am not confident.

☹ I don't understand and this is difficult.

Learning objective	☺	😐	☹
Reading skills			
I can use my knowledge of letters and sounds to read words.			
I can choose the right story language to complete a sentence.			
Writing skills			
I can answer questions about the story.			
I can write what I like or don't like about the story.			
I can say what might happen next in a story.			
I can add missing capital letters and full stops to sentences.			
I can add missing words and phrases to sentences.			
Language (spelling) skills			
I can find and write words that have the /**oo**/ sound.			
I can find and write words that have the /**ow**/ sound.			

(5) Water world

A–Z of the Sea

Read this text and look at the pictures. The glossary on page 89 will help you understand any difficult words, for example **bristles**.

Aa

albatross

A large bird with long wings that can fly far across oceans.

Arctic Ocean

The world's smallest ocean around the cold North Pole.

Bb

baleen whale

A kind of whale that does not have teeth. It has lots of soft **bristles** in its mouth (called baleen) which hang down and allow food to pass through them.

baleen

beach

Land by the sea made of sand or **pebbles**.

blubber

Fat under the skin of seals and other sea animals that keeps them warm in cold seas.

Cc

cave

A big hole in a cliff.

cliff

A steep hill made of rock next to the sea.

coast

The land that is right next to the sea.

cliff

beach

coral

A type of rock in the sea that is made from the **skeletons** of tiny creatures.

crab

An animal that has a hard shell on its back and **powerful** claws. It lives in the sea.

Dd

dolphin

A large mammal that swims like a fish, breathes air and does not have **gills**.

dugong

A **mammal** that lives in the Pacific and Indian Oceans. It is called a 'sea cow' because it eats grass under the water.

A–Z of the Sea

A Now answer these questions about the text.

1 Draw lines to link the pictures with their labels.

dugong   **albatross**   **crab**   **coral**

2 Read this information.

beach   Land by the sea made of sand or pebbles.

What sort of book is this information from?

a story book ☐

a dictionary ☐

a comic book ☐

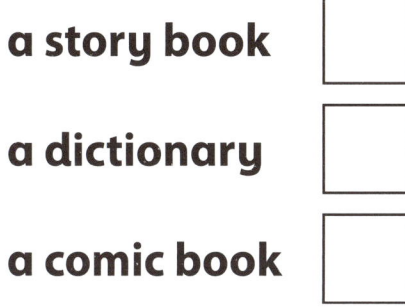

Learning tip
A dictionary has information in A to Z order.

B

1 Finish the sentence by choosing one of the endings in the box.

Seals have blubber because

_____

it smells good	**it keeps them cool**
it helps them swim	**it keeps them warm**

C

1 Name four living things from the text.

_____   _____

_____   _____

2 Choose one. Write a sentence to say what it is.

_____

_____

Word detective

A Choose the missing words to fill the gaps.

> **and   a   the**

Crab: An animal that has _____ **hard shell on its back**

_____ **powerful claws. It lives in** _____ **sea.**

B Find three words from page 45 that begin with **c**. Write them on the crab.

C Find these words from *A–Z of the Sea* in the word search.

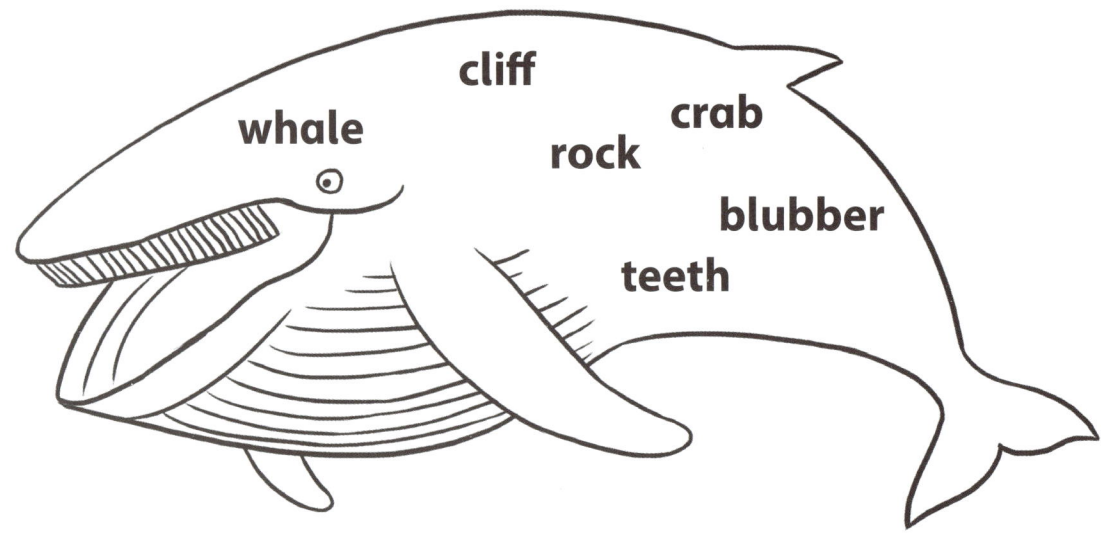

whale   cliff   crab   rock   blubber   teeth

a	o	c	r	a	b	e
p	r	o	s	v	z	h
g	w	x	z	w	s	h
e	h	k	r	o	c	k
n	a	c	l	i	f	f
b	l	u	b	b	e	r
t	e	e	t	h	x	v

Write the word that means 'a steep hill made of rock next to

the sea' _____

Get writing

Part 1

Write the correct mark at the end of each sentence.

> **Language tip**
> A full stop **.** ends a sentence.
> A question mark **?** comes at the end of a question.

Is it a whale _____

Yes, it's a baleen whale _____

Part 2

Write the question words for these questions.

1. _____ **is the Arctic?**   **It is around the cold North Pole.**

2. _____ **is a cave?**   **It is a big hole in a cliff.**

Part 3

Write some questions for a quiz about sea transport.

Choose a word from the box to start each question.

Where   What   Who

Learning tip
Remember – the question and answer should make sense together.

____What____ is used to push a canoe along?

Answer: A paddle

_____ were dragon boats first made?

Answer: China

_____ were the first people to use sails?

Answer: The ancient Egyptians

_____ is at the front of a dragon boat?

Answer: A carved dragon head

Check my learning

Unit 5 Water world

Name _____   Date _____

☺ I understand and I can do this well.

😐 I understand but I am not confident.

☹ I don't understand and this is difficult.

Learning objective	☺	😐	☹
Reading skills			
I can use my knowledge of letters and sounds to read words.			
I can read and understand a glossary.			
I can write the meaning of a word for a dictionary.			
Writing skills			
I can choose and write the correct words and phrases to finish sentences.			
I can write the correct mark at the end of sentences.			
Language (spelling) skills			
I can find and write words that begin with 'c'.			
I can write question words.			

6 Creatures big and small

Read this poem out loud.

The Flea

Jump
   Jump
It's a flea, a flea!
Can you see?

It's on that leaf.
It's watching me.
It's a **teeny** flea
    with jumping legs
      a tiny head
      and teeth that BITE.
It's jumping near,
    nearer still.
It's time to flee,
From that
   teeny
      tiny
        jumping
         BITING flea!

Liz Miles

Now answer these questions about the poem.

A How big is the flea? Circle the answer.

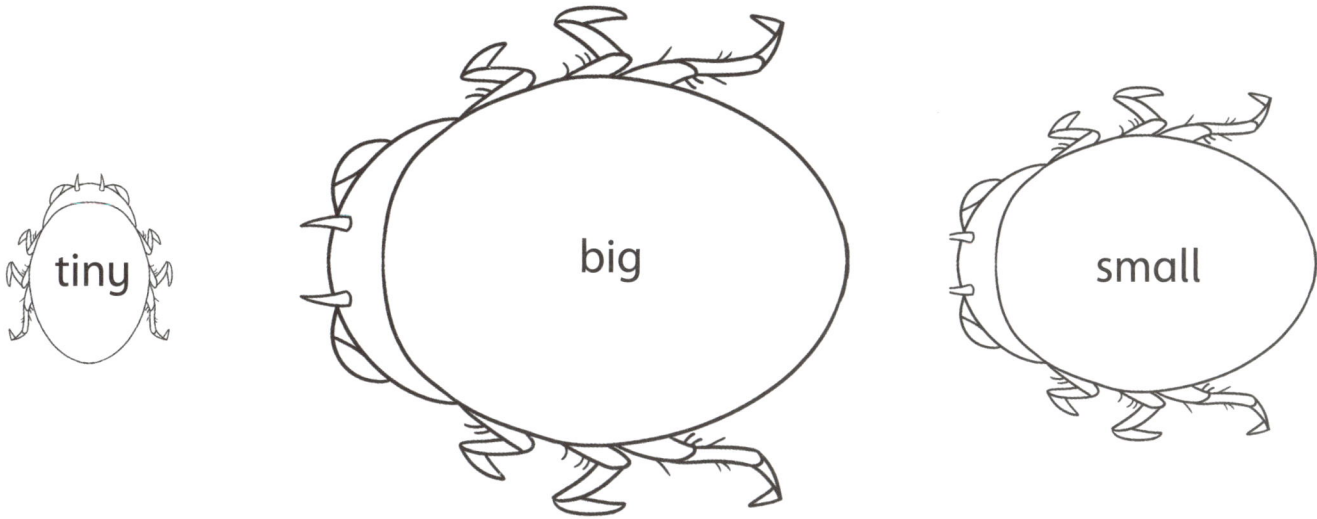

tiny

big

small

B Say the words aloud. Underline two words that rhyme with flea.

> time   me   that   legs   flee   jump

Learning tip
Read the words aloud to hear which words have the /**ee**/ sound.

C What is the boy scared of?

the flea's legs ☐   **the flea's wings** ☐   **the flea's teeth** ☐

Word detective 🔍

A Answer these questions about **–ing** words.

1 Circle the words with the **–ing** ending.

> **buzzing   flying   nearer   eating   legs**

2 Find a word in the poem with the **–ing** ending. Write it down.

_____

3 Add **–ing** to these words. Say the words aloud.

help _____   **sing** _____

wish _____   **catch** _____

B Find two words in 'The Flea' that mean **very small**.

C Find these words from 'The Flea' in the word search.

near   flea   tiny   leaf
jumping   teeth   me   flee

p	n	e	a	r	f	t
m	h	a	n	f	m	e
t	i	n	y	l	o	e
j	a	f	l	e	e	t
w	c	g	v	a	k	h
j	u	m	p	i	n	g
l	e	a	f	i	s	o

Which word means **to run away**? _____.

One, two, three, four, five

Read this rhyme out loud.

One, two, three, four, five,
Once I caught a fish alive.
Six, seven, eight, nine, ten,
Then I let it go again.

Why did you let it go?
Because it bit my finger so.
Which finger did it bite?
This little finger on the right.

Learning tip

Number words

1 one	2 two	3 three	4 four	5 five
6 six	7 seven	8 eight	9 nine	10 ten

Now answer these questions about the rhyme.

A Why did the boy let the fish go? Tick the correct answer.

The fish bit the boy. ☐

The boy bit the fish. ☐

The fish fell. ☐

B Which finger did the fish bite?

left little finger ☐   **right little finger** ☐

Word detective

A Draw lines to connect the words that rhyme.

go	alive
five	so
bite	right

Learning tip
Read the words aloud to hear which words sound the same.

Get writing

Use one of the rhyming words below to finish each line.

door   sun   tree   two   four

Five little bats were hanging from a _____

One flew off and then there were ____four____ .

Four little bats were playing in a _____

One fluttered off and then there were three.

Three little bats in the moon so blue

One flapped off and then there were _____ .

Two little bats were having such fun

One fell asleep and then there was one.

Quick! Go to bed – it's the morning _____ !

Check my learning

Unit 6 Creatures big and small

Name _____   Date _____

😊 I understand and I can do this well.

😐 I understand but I am not confident.

☹ I don't understand and this is difficult.

Learning objective	😊	😐	☹
Reading skills			
I can read words aloud to hear which words rhyme.			
I can answer questions about the poems I have read.			
Writing skills			
I can underline words that rhyme.			
I can draw lines to connect rhyming words.			
I can write my own poem by finishing lines with rhyming words.			
Language (spelling) skills			
I can write words that end with **–ing**.			

 Stories about our world

Read the opening to a story called *Alien at School*.

It was a dark, dark night. The little school was shut and all the children were in bed, asleep. Everyone in the village was asleep, except for a pony. He was **munching** some straw under a tree, enjoying the peace.

Suddenly, there was a flash of light. The pony stopped eating and listened. Zoom! The light got brighter and brighter; the zoom got louder and louder. A rocket with a bright green light shot lower and lower.

Down and down went the rocket, until … splash! It landed in a pond next to the school gate.

The pony **pretended** to be busy munching as the door of the rocket opened. A little alien stepped out. She was as tall as the pony and wore a yellow dress with red spots. Her skin was green and she had eyes on stalks.

"Ooh!" she said. "A school! This will be fun. I want to learn to read!" She tapped the gate with a silver stick and said, "Open!" The gate opened.

1 Colour the alien so that it looks like the alien in the story.

Learning tip
Check the story to find the colours for the alien's dress and skin.

2 What did the alien do with her stick?

_____

_____

B

1 Where did the rocket land?

_____

2 Why was the alien excited to see a school?

She wanted to meet the school children.

She had never seen a school before.

She wanted to learn to read.

She was really good at reading.

 C

1 How do you think the children will feel when they go to school and see the alien?

2 How do you think the alien will feel, being new at school? Circle the words.

> nervous   excited   scared   happy

3 How can the children make her feel welcome?

_____

_____

Word detective

 A

1 Read the words below.

> eating   green   alien   pony
> night   dark   tree

2 Write the words from the story with the /**ee**/ sound around the rocket.

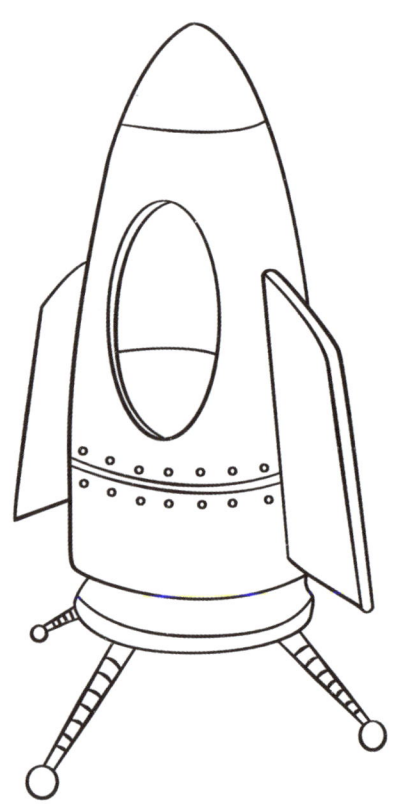

Learning tip
Don't forget that the /**ee**/ sound can be spelled **ee**, **ea** and **y**.

B Find these words from *Alien at School* in the word search and circle them.

rocket   night   pond   bed   splash   dress

c	d	y	s	r	p
x	r	w	p	o	o
b	e	d	l	c	n
g	s	r	a	k	d
b	s	p	s	e	f
n	i	g	h	t	n

C

1 Read the words aloud.

2 Circle the word with the /**sh**/ sound.

3 Write the word that means the opposite of **day**.

Get writing ✏️

Part 1

Story sentences

Finish the sentences under the pictures.

The children were in __bed__ .

The little alien t__pped the gate.

There was a fl_____ of light.

The rocket landed in a p_____ .

A little a_____ stepped out.   **"This will be f_____ ."**

Part 2

Ordering events

Order the events in **Part 1** by numbering them 1–6.

The first two have been done for you.

Check my learning

Unit 7 Stories about our world

Name _____ Date _____

☺ I understand and I can do this well.

😐 I understand but I am not confident.

☹ I don't understand and this is difficult.

Learning objective	☺	😐	☹
Reading skills			
I can use my knowledge of letters and sounds to read words.			
I can order the events in a story.			
Writing skills			
I can answer questions about the story.			
I can add missing words to finish sentences.			
Language (spelling) skills			
I can find and write words that have the /**ee**/ sound.			
I can find and write a word that has the /**sh**/ sound.			
I can find and write a word that means the opposite of **day**.			

8 About my life

Read about a class's trip to a wildlife park.

Our Class Trip to the Wildlife Park

Last Friday, Mrs Tong and Mr Khan took our class on a trip. We went to the wildlife park.

We got to school at 8 o'clock to get on the coach. We had to bring a drink and a snack for lunch. Mrs Tong got cross because Rosa was late. The coach had to wait ten more minutes.

At 9 o'clock, the coach got to the wildlife park. The park warden told us to read the rules.

Next, we split into two groups. Rosa and I went in Mrs Tong's group. After going up lots of steps, we saw the lions. After a short walk we saw a tiger, too.

Then the park **warden** let us feed a baby giraffe. Rosa jumped because it licked her arm.

At lunchtime, we sat near the lake. Then we went to a shack for ice creams. Next, we followed signs to the bathrooms.

During the afternoon we went to see the hippos in the mud, then the pandas.

Finally we went into a shop. I got a panda balloon.

While we waited for the coach, we played on swings. At last the bus came. We got to school by 4 o'clock. We thanked the driver and our teachers for a **brilliant** day.

A What is the name of the wildlife park?

_____

_____

Learning tip
Look for information in the pictures.

B Draw lines to match the times to the sentences.

10 past 8

lunchtime

They got to the wildlife park.

They got back to school.

The coach set off.

They sat by the lake.

9 o'clock

4 o'clock

1 Did the writer enjoy the day? Circle Yes or No.

Yes   No

What word did they use to describe the day?

_____

2 What animal would you like to visit at a wildlife park?
Write the animal on the first line. Choose one of the words below
to complete the second sentence.

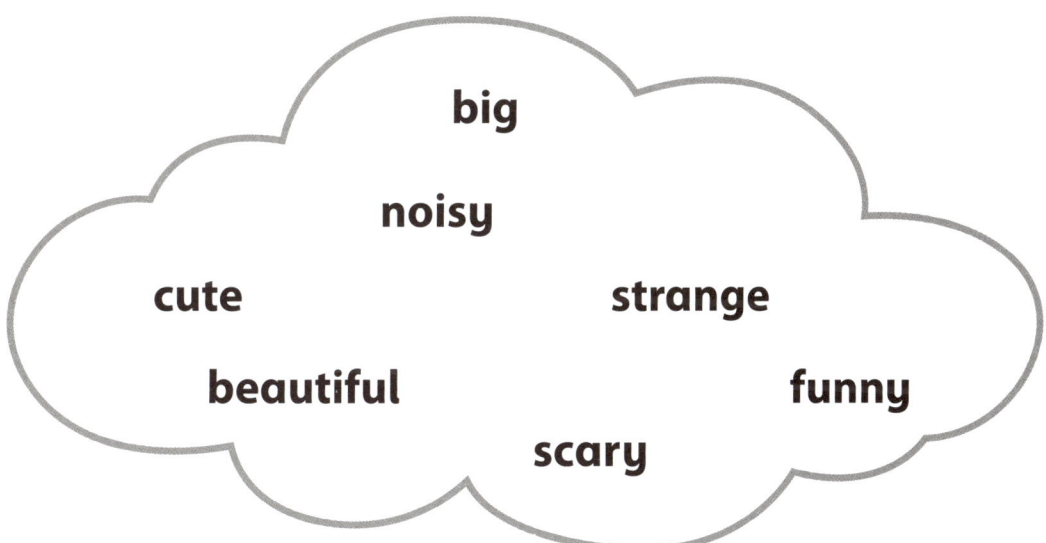

big

noisy

cute   strange

beautiful   funny

scary

I would like to visit the _____

because they are _____ .

Word detective

A

1 Draw a line to link the labels to the correct animals at the wildlife park.

hippo

giraffe

lion

tiger

panda

2 Which animal did the class see first?

_____

3 Add numbers to show the order in which the class saw the animals.

1 Find these words in the word search and circle them.

then   next   finally   after   lunch

w	h	l	u	n	c	h
a	n	e	x	t	s	f
o	c	t	c	k	k	h
f	i	n	a	l	l	y
k	t	h	e	n	i	z
u	v	a	f	t	e	r

2 Write the word with the /**ch**/ sound.

_____

3 Which word means **at the end**?

_____

1 Write the correct labels for each animal at the wildlife park.

hippos   giraffes   pandas   lions   tigers

g_____

t_____

lake

ice cream shack

h_____

l_____

p_____

ZOO

parrots

shop

seals

entrance

2 Draw a line on the map to show Rosa's route around the wildlife park.

Get writing

Imagine you went to the wildlife park. Fill the gaps in the sentences with words from the map or boxes below. Some words have been started for you.

giraffes **tigers** **seals** **pandas** **parrots**	**lunch** **snack** **drink**	**First** **Next**

We got to the wildlife park at 10 o'clock. F _____ ,

we went to see the lions. N _____ ,

we went to see the _____ . After a

dr _____ and a sn_____ , we

went to see the _____ .

At 1 o'clock, we sat near the lake and had _____ .

In the afternoon, we saw hippos and _____ .

We got back to school at 4 o'clock.

Check my learning

Unit 8 About my life

Name _____   Date _____

☺ I understand and I can do this well.

😐 I understand but I am not confident.

☹ I don't understand and this is difficult.

Learning objective	☺	😐	☹
Reading skills			
I can use my knowledge of letters and sounds to read words.			
I can read and understand a map.			
Writing skills			
I can answer questions about the text.			
I can find and link words that tell you when something happened.			
I can write labels for animals at a wildlife park.			
I can add words to finish a text about a trip to a wildlife park.			
Language (spelling) skills			
I can find and write a word that has the /**ch**/ sound.			
I can write an adverbial of time that means **at the end**.			

9 Poems that tell a story

Read this extract from a poem about a family's holiday to Mexico.

We circle round the plaza and we hear the stamping feet. As dancers **twirl**, their costumes swirl To the guitarists' beat.

We **hike** up to the winter home of the monarch butterflies. When sunshine brings a burst of wings, Their glitter fills the skies.

Laurie Krebs

Now answer these questions about the text.

A What do the family hear first?
Circle the answer.

> guitars   stamping feet   a butterfly's wings

B

1 What does **hike** mean in this line? Tick the correct answer.
We hike up to the winter home of the monarch butterflies.

fly in a plane ☐   **ride bikes** ☐   **walk** ☐

2 What does it mean when it says the dancer's costumes **swirl**?

The costumes move around. ☐

The costumes stay still. ☐

The costumes have a pattern on them. ☐

C

1 Underline the word that means
shiny and bright.
Their glitter fills the skies

2 Which verse on page 81 do you like best? Explain why.

I like the _____ **verse best because** _____

_____

Word detective

A Find two /**ee**/ words in the poem and write them in the clouds.

ee word

Language tip
Remember, words with the /**ee**/ sound can be spelt **ee** or **ea**.

ea word

Read this poem aloud.

Family holiday

Gran wants to go where the river is deep,
To hide in the shadows and
Watch the crocodiles sleep.

Mum wants the peace of the woodland trees,
To climb up a trunk and
Swing in the breeze.

Dad wants to go where the sky is blue,
To sit on a beach, then
Cook a barbecue.

I want to climb up that mountain-top,
Go to the café and
Buy a lollipop!

A Who likes the sea? Tick the correct answer.

Mum ☐   **Dad** ☐   **Gran** ☐

B Why does Mum like the woodland?

It is noisy. ☐   **It is peaceful.** ☐   **It is hot.** ☐

Word detective

Draw lines to connect the words that rhyme.

sleep	**trees**
breeze	**deep**
blue	**barbecue**

Language tip
Rhyming words don't always have the same spelling.

Get writing

Write your own poem about people in your family and what they might do on holiday.

Part 1

Choose some rhyming words to use in your poem. You can use the words in the box. Use names of your family in your poem.

sea	free	me	see	cup	up	fun	sun	sand
hand	dinner	winner	away	say	day	play

_____

_____

_____

_____

_____

_____

When you have written your poem, read it aloud to a partner or an adult.

Part 2

Think of a title for your family holiday poem.

My family holiday poem is called _____

Draw a picture to go with your poem.

Check my learning

Unit 9 Poems that tell a story

Name _____   Date _____

😊 I understand and I can do this well.

😐 I understand but I am not confident.

☹ I don't understand and this is difficult.

Learning objective	😊	😐	☹
Reading skills			
I can use my knowledge of letters and sounds to read words.			
I understand the meaning of **hike** and **swirl**.			
I can explain why I like a verse of a poem best.			
I can find pairs of words that rhyme.			
Writing skills			
I can finish a poem about my family.			
I can write a title for my poem.			
Language (spelling) skills			
I can write and spell the names of people in my family.			
I can find and spell words with **ee** and **ea** spellings.			

Glossary

Bb

bow *verb* to bend forward to show respect

brilliant *adjective* something that is very good

bristles *noun* short, stiff hairs

Cc

coast *noun* the land that is right next
　　to the sea

Gg

gills *noun* the parts on the sides of a fish
　　that it breathes through

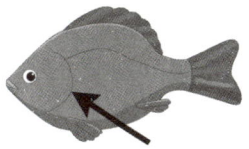

Hh

hike *verb* to go for a long walk in the countryside

Mm

mammal *noun* an animal that gives birth to live babies
　　and feeds its young with its own milk

munching *verb* chewing something noisily

Pp

pebbles *noun* small, smooth stones you find on
　　the beach

polite *adjective* when someone has good manners and is
　　not rude to people

poppadoms *noun* large circular pieces of thin, fried bread

powerful *adjective* very strong

pretended *verb* acted as though something was true when it was not really

Ss

serious *adjective* very important

skeletons *noun* the bones that hold up the body of a person or animal

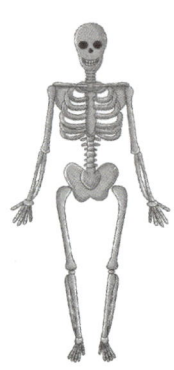

Tt

teeny *adjective* very small

twirl *verb* to spin round and round

Ww

warden *noun* someone who supervises something

100 High frequency words

a	am	cat	to	I
it	the	dog	big	on
mum	up	dad	we	me
and	my	at	for	he
is	no	can	all	get
in	go	was	of	day
she	see	like	yes	look
come	went	you	are	said
this	going	they	away	play
so	but	as	an	do

did	be	bed	his	him
her	ran	put	not	from
had	has	got	dig	been
us	seen	saw	if	or
by	boy	girl	good	may
will	man	help	ball	door
push	pull	over	much	must
now	off	way	have	how
home	house	came	time	last
jump	just	after	out	tree

Key words to help you at school

challenge *noun* something difficult that someone has to do

"I accept your challenge," said the knight.

connect *verb* to join things together

You need to connect the printer to your computer.

diagram *noun* a drawing or picture that shows the parts of something or how it works

Your diagram of the car is great!

explore *verb* to examine something or somewhere carefully

We need to explore this subject.

familiar *adjective* knowing something well

Are you familiar with the story?

imagine *verb* to form a picture of something or someone in your mind

I close my eyes and imagine a beach.

information *noun* facts or what someone tells you

Here is some information about cats.

introduction *noun* words at the beginning of a book, explaining what it is about

The introduction was funny.

knowledge *noun* what someone or everybody knows

Here is a quiz to test our knowledge.

label *verb* to add information to something

Please label your diagram.

organise *verb* 1. to plan or arrange something

We're organising a picnic.

2. to put things in order

Let's organise your drawers.

practise *verb* to do something often so that you get better at it

Please practise your reading every night.

predict *verb* to say that something will happen in the future

I predict it is going to be sunny today.

review *noun* a description and opinion of a book, film, play or piece of music

He wrote a review of the book.

understand *verb* to know what something means or how it works

I understand how to make the model now.